Easy & Delicious

Donut Cookbook

Simple Donut Recipes for the Beginner

BY: Nancy Silverman

COPYRIGHT NOTICES

IIIIIIIIIIIIIIIIIIIIIIIIIIIIIIIIIIIIIIIIIIIIIIIIIIIIIIIIIIIIIIIIIII

My Heartfelt Thanks and A Special Reward for Your Purchase!

Subsribe now!

Enter your email | Subscribe

https://nancy.gr8.com

My heartfelt thanks at purchasing my book and I hope you enjoy it! As a special bonus, you will now be eligible to receive books absolutely free on a weekly basis! Get started by entering your email address in the box above to subscribe. A notification will be emailed to you of my free promotions, no purchase necessary! With little effort, you will be eligible for free and discounted books daily. In addition to this amazing gift, a reminder will be sent 1-2 days before the offer expires to remind you not to miss out. Enter now to start enjoying this special offer!

Table of Contents

(1) Baked Lemon Donuts

These are the perfect donuts for you to make whenever you are craving something sweet and fresh. They are perfect to make during the hot summer months.

Serving Sizes: 6 servings

Preparation Time: 25 minutes

Ingredients for the donuts:

- 1 egg, beaten
- ¾ cup of white sugar
- 6 ounces of plain Greek yogurt
- ¼ cup of canola oil
- 1 Tablespoon of lemon zest
- 1 Tablespoon of lemon extract
- 3 to 5 drops of yellow food coloring
- 1 ¼ cups of all-purpose flour
- ½ teaspoon of baking powder
- ½ teaspoon of baking soda
- ¼ teaspoon of salt

Ingredients for the glaze:

- 1 cup of powdered sugar
- 3 tablespoons of lemon juice

IIIIIIIIIIIIIIIIIIIIIIIIIIIIIIIIIIIIIIIIIIIIIIIIIIIIIIIIIIIIIII

Instructions:

1. Preheat the oven to 350 degrees. Grease a large donut pan with cooking spray.

2. In a large bowl, add in the beaten egg, white sugar, plain yogurt, canola oil, lemon zest, lemon extract and drops of yellow food coloring. Whisk until smooth in consistency.

3. Add in the all-purpose flour, dash of salt, baking powder and soda. Stir well until just mixed.

4. Pour the batter into the greased donut pan. Place into the oven to bake for 15 to 17 minutes or until golden brown. Remove and place the donuts onto a wire rack to cool completely.

5. In a small bowl, add in the powdered sugar and lemon juice. Whisk until smooth in consistency.

6. Dip the tops of the donuts in the glaze. Place back onto the wire rack to set for 5 minutes before serving.

(2) Baked Apple Donuts

This is the perfect donut recipe to prepare during the fall months. It is so delicious, you can serve them for your Thanksgiving dinner to serve your family and friends a special treat.

Serving Sizes: 22 to 24 servings

Preparation Time: 25 minutes

Ingredients for the donuts:

- 4 cups of all-purpose flour
- 4 teaspoons of baking powder
- 1 ½ teaspoon of salt
- ½ teaspoon of baking soda
- 1 ½ Tablespoon of ground cinnamon
- ¼ teaspoon of ground nutmeg
- ¼ cup of unsalted butter, melted and cooled
- 2 eggs, beaten lightly
- 1 cup of white sugar
- ½ cup of buttermilk
- 1 cup of unsweetened applesauce
- 1 ½ cup of apple, peeled and grated

Ingredients for the coating:

- Unsweetened applesauce, as needed
- 1 cup of white sugar
- 1 Tablespoon of ground cinnamon
- Dash of ground nutmeg, optional

|||||||||||||||||||||||||||||||||||||||||||||||||||||||||||||||||||

Instructions:

1. Preheat the oven to 375 degrees.

2. In a large bowl, add in the all-purpose flour, dash of salt, ground cinnamon, ground nutmeg, baking powder and soda. Stir well to mix.

3. In a separate large bowl, add in the melted butter, beaten eggs, white sugar, buttermilk and unsweetened applesauce. Add in the grated apple and stir well to mix.

4. Add the flour mixture into the butter mixture. Stir well until just mixed.

5. Pour the batter into a large greased donut pan. Place into the oven to bake for 12 to 15 minutes at 375 degrees or until golden brown. Remove and transfer the donuts onto a wire rack to cool completely.

6. In a small bowl, add in the remaining cup of white sugar, tablespoon of ground cinnamon and ground nutmeg. Stir well to mix.

7. Brush the extra applesauce over each donut and dip into the cinnamon mixture. Serve immediately.

(3) Glaze Chocolate Donuts

To kick things off, we have these deliciously glazed chocolate donuts for those who have a strong sweet tooth that needs to be satisfied. Serve these donuts with freshly brewed coffee for the tastiest results.

Serving Sizes: 10 servings

Preparation Time: 20 minutes

Ingredients for the donuts:

- 1 cup of all-purpose flour
- ½ cup of sugar
- ¼ cup of powdered cocoa
- ¼ cup of miniature chocolate chips, optional
- ½ teaspoon of baking soda
- ¼ teaspoon of salt
- ½ teaspoon of pure vanilla
- 1 egg, large
- 6 tablespoons of sour cream
- ¼ cup of whole milk
- ¼ cup of vegetable oil

Ingredients for the glaze:

- 1 ½ cups of powdered sugar
- ¼ cup of whole milk
- 1 teaspoon of pure vanilla

IIIIIIIIIIIIIIIIIIIIIIIIIIIIIIIIIIIIIIIIIIIIIIIIIIIIIIIIIIIIIIIIIIIIIIII

Instructions:

1. Preheat the oven to 375 degrees. Grease a large donut pan with cooking spray

2. In a medium bowl, add in the all-purpose flour, white sugar, powdered cocoa, miniature chocolate chips and baking soda. Stir well to mix.

3. In a separate small bowl, add in the pure vanilla, large egg, sour cream, whole milk and vegetable oil. Stir well until evenly blended.

4. Add the vanilla mixture into the flour mixture. Stir well until mixed.

5. Pour the batter into the prepared donut pan.

6. Place into the oven to bake for 8 to 10 minutes or until cooked through. Remove and remove the donuts from the pan. Set onto a wire rack to cool completely.

7. In a medium bowl, add in the powdered sugar, whole milk and pure vanilla. Stir well until smooth in consistency.

8. Dunk the donuts completely into the glaze and place onto a wire rack for 5 minutes or until the glaze is set.

(4) Red Velvet Donuts

These are the perfect donuts to make whenever you are looking for a classy donut to make to impress your friends and family. It is so easy to make, it can be ready on your table in 30 minutes or less.

Serving Sizes: 8 to 10 servings

Preparation Time: 30 minutes

Ingredients for the donuts:

- 1 cup of all-purpose flour
- 1 Tablespoon of powdered cocoa, unsweetened
- ½ cup of white sugar
- 1 teaspoon of baker's style baking powder
- ½ teaspoon of baker's style baking soda
- ¼ teaspoon of salt
- 2 eggs, beaten
- 1 teaspoon of red food coloring
- 3 tablespoons of buttermilk
- 3 tablespoons of vegetable oil
- ½ teaspoon of pure vanilla

Ingredients for the glaze:

- ¼ cup of cream cheese, soft
- ½ cup of powdered sugar
- ½ teaspoon of pure vanilla
- 2 tablespoons of whole milk

|||||||||||||||||||||||||||||||||||||||||||||||||||||||||||||||||||||

Instructions:

1. In a medium bowl, add in the all-purpose flour, powdered cocoa, white sugar, dash of salt, baking powder and soda. Stir well to mix.

2. In a separate medium bowl, add in the beaten eggs, vegetable oil, buttermilk and red food coloring. Beat with an electric mixer on the medium setting until foamy. Pour this mixture into the flour mixture. Stir until just mixed.

3. Preheat the oven to 375 degrees. Grease a large donut pan with cooking spray.

4. Pour the donut batter into the greased donut pan. Place into the oven to bake for 8 to 10 minutes or until golden brown. Remove and transfer onto a wire rack to cool completely.

5. In a medium bowl of a stand mixer, add in the powdered sugar, soft cream cheese, pure vanilla and whole milk. Beat until smooth in consistency.

6. Dip the tops of the donuts into the glaze. Set on the wire rack to set for 5 minutes before serving.

(5) Double Chocolate Donuts

These donuts are every chocolate lovers dream. Chocolate donuts topped off with chocolate frosting, these are the types of donuts that people of all ages are going to love.

Serving Sizes: 8 servings

Preparation Time: 25 minutes

Ingredients for the donuts:

- ¾ cup of all-purpose flour
- 1/3 cup of powdered cocoa
- ½ teaspoon of baking soda
- ¼ teaspoon of salt
- 2 ½ Tablespoon of butter, melted
- 1 egg, beaten
- ¼ cup of light brown sugar
- 3 tablespoons of white sugar
- 1 ½ teaspoon of pure vanilla
- 2/3 cup of buttermilk

Ingredients for the glaze:

- ¾ cup of powdered sugar
- 3 tablespoons of powdered cocoa
- 3 to 4 tablespoons of heavy whipping cream
- 2 teaspoons of corn syrup
- Rainbow sprinkles, for topping and optional

||||||||||||||||||||||||||||||||||||||||||||||||||||||||||||||

Instructions:

1. Preheat the oven to 350 degrees. Grease a large donut pan with cooking spray.

2. In a medium bowl, add in the all-purpose flour, powdered cocoa, dash of salt and baking soda. Stir well to mix.

3. In a separate medium bowl, add in the melted butter, beaten egg, white sugar, pure vanilla and butter milk. Stir well to mix and pour into the flour mixture. Stir well until just mixed.

4. Pour the batter into the greased donut pan. Place into the oven to bake for 8 to 10 minutes or until baked through. Remove and transfer the donuts onto a wire rack to cool completely.

5. In a small bowl, add in the remaining ¾ cup of powdered sugar, powdered cocoa, heavy whipping cream and corn syrup. Whisk until smooth in consistency.

6. Dip the tops of the donuts in the glaze. Sprinkle the rainbow sprinkles over the top.

7. Place back onto a wire rack to set for 5 minutes before serving.

(6) Chocolate and Peanut Butter Donuts

If you love chocolate and peanut butter, then this are donuts that I know you will want to make as often as possible. It is so delicious; chocolate lovers will love these donuts.

Serving Sizes: 20 servings

Preparation Time: 20 minutes

Ingredients for the donuts:

- 2 cups of all-purpose flour
- ¾ cup of powdered cocoa
- 1 teaspoon of baking soda
- ½ teaspoon of salt
- 1 cup of light brown sugar
- 1 cup of buttermilk
- 2 eggs, beaten
- ½ cup of butter, melted
- 2 teaspoons of pure vanilla

Ingredients for the glaze:

- 1 ½ cup of powdered sugar
- 3 tablespoons of powdered cocoa
- 3 to 4 tablespoons of peanut butter
- 4 to 5 tablespoons of whole milk
- 2 teaspoons of pure vanilla

IIIIIIIIIIIIIIIIIIIIIIIIIIIIIIIIIIIIIIIIIIIIIIIIIIIIIIIIIIIIIIII

Instructions:

1. Preheat an oven to 325 degrees. Grease a large donut pan with cooking spray.

2. In a large bowl, add in the all-purpose flour, powdered cocoa, baking soda, light brown sugar and dash of salt.

3. In a separate medium bowl, add in the buttermilk, beaten eggs, melted butter and pure vanilla. Stir well to mix and add into the flour mixture. Stir until just mixed.

4. Pour the batter into the greased donut pan. Place into the oven to bake for 10 to 13 minutes. Remove and place the donuts onto a wire rack to cool completely.

5. In a small bowl, add in ¼ cup of the peanut butter. Microwave for 30 seconds or until melted.

6. In a separate small bowl, add in all of the ingredients for the glaze. Whisk until smooth in consistency.

7. Dip the tops of the donuts into the chocolate glaze. Drizzle the peanut butter over the top of the donuts. Serve immediately.

(7) Birthday Cake Donuts

Just as the name implies, this is a donut dish you can make just in time for your friends or family member's birthday. It tastes exactly like a birthday cake, making it one of the best and most delicious donuts you will ever taste.

Serving Sizes: 8 servings

Preparation Time: 30 minutes

Ingredients for the donuts:

- 1 teaspoon of baking powder
- ¼ teaspoon of baking soda
- 1 cup of all-purpose flour
- ¼ teaspoon of salt
- ¼ teaspoon of ground nutmeg
- ¼ cup of white sugar
- 1 Tablespoon of light brown sugar
- ¼ cup of whole milk
- ¼ cup of Greek yogurt
- 1 egg, large
- 2 tablespoons of unsalted butter, melted
- 1 ½ teaspoon of pure vanilla
- ½ cup of rainbow sprinkles

Ingredients for the glaze:

- ¼ cup of whole milk
- 2 cups of confectioner's sugar
- 1 teaspoon of pure vanilla
- Rainbow sprinkles, for topping and optional

|||||||||||||||||||||||||||||||||||||||||||||||||||||||||||||||||||||

Instructions:

1. Preheat the oven to 350 degrees. Grease a large donut pan with cooking spray.

2. In a medium bowl, add in the all-purpose flour, dash of salt, ground nutmeg, white sugar, light brown sugar, baking powder and soda. Stir well to mix and set the mixture aside.

3. In a separate large bowl, add in the whole milk, Greek yogurt and large egg. Stir well until smooth in consistency. Add in the melted butter and pure vanilla. Stir again until evenly mixed.

4. Pour the milk mixture into the flour mixture. Stir until just mixed.

5. Pour the batter into the prepared donut pan.

7. Place into the oven to bake for 8 to 10 minutes or until the donuts are golden. Remove and set the donuts onto a wire rack to cool completely.

8. In a medium saucepan set over low heat, add in the remaining ¼ cup of milk, powdered sugar and pure vanilla. Whisk until smooth in consistency. Remove from heat.

9. Dip the tops of the donuts into the glaze and transfer back to the wire rack.

10. Sprinkle the rainbow sprinkles over the top and allow to set for 5 minutes before serving.

(8) Classic Glazed Donuts

This is a classic donut recipe you can make as a special treat to serve to your family in the morning. Paired excellently with a fresh cup of coffee, I know you won't be able to get enough of these classic donuts.

Serving Sizes: 12 servings

Preparation Time: 1 hour and 20 minutes

Ingredients for the donuts:

- 2 packs of yeast
- ¼ cup of warm water
- 1 ½ cups of warm milk
- ½ cup of sugar
- 1 teaspoon of salt
- 2 eggs, beaten
- ½ cup of shortening
- 5 cups of all-purpose flour
- 4 cups of vegetable oil

Ingredients for the glaze:

- 2 ½ cups of powdered sugar
- ¼ cup of whole milk
- ¼ cup of corn syrup

||||||||||||||||||||||||||||||||||||||||||||||||||||||||||||||||||

Instructions:

1. In a large bowl of a stand mixer, add in the water and yeast packets. Stir to mix and set aside for 10 minutes.

2. Add in the whole milk, white sugar, dash of salt, beaten eggs, shortening and 2 cups of all-purpose flour. Stir until just mixed. Add in the remaining dough and stir well until smooth.

3. Cover the dough and set aside to rise for 1 hour.

4. Punch down the dough and roll the dough on a flat surface that has been dusted with flour until ½ inch in thickness. Cut out donut shapes using a donut cutter and set onto a large baking sheet lined with wax paper.

5. Set aside to rise for 35 to 40 minutes.

6. In a large cast iron pot set over medium heat, add in the four cups of vegetable oil. Once the oil begins to shimmer, add in the donuts. Fry the donuts for 1 minute on each side or until golden brown. Remove and place onto a large plate lined with paper towels to drain.

7. In a small bowl, add in the powdered sugar, whole milk and corn syrup. Whisk until smooth in consistency.

8. Dunk the donuts completely in the glaze. Set onto the baking sheet to rest for 5 minutes or until the glaze is set. Serve.

(9) Apple Cider Vinegar Donuts

These are the perfect donuts to make if you are looking for something on the healthier side. These donuts are paleo friendly, gluten free and low in calories, making it perfect for everybody, regardless on the kind of diet they are on.

Serving Sizes: 8 servings

Preparation Time: 25 minutes

Ingredients for the donuts:

- 4 eggs, beaten
- 4 tablespoons of coconut oil, melted
- 3 tablespoons of honey
- 2/3 cup of apple cider vinegar
- 1 cup of coconut flour
- 1 teaspoon of ground cinnamon
- 1 teaspoon of baking soda
- Dash of salt
- Pumpkin coffee syrup, for drizzling

|||||||||||||||||||||||||||||||||||||||||||||||||||||||||||||

Instructions:

1. Preheat the oven to 350 degrees. Grease a large donut pan with cooking spray.

2. In a small bowl, add in the beaten eggs, dash of salt, honey, vinegar and melted coconut oil. Stir well until evenly mixed.

3. In a separate medium bowl, add in the ground cinnamon, coconut flour and baking soda. Stir well until mixed. Add in the egg mixture and stir well until the mixture is just mixed.

4. Pour the batter into the greased donut pan. Place into the oven to bake for 8 to 10 minutes or until golden brown. Remove and transfer onto a wire rack to cool completely.

5. Drizzle the pumpkin coffee syrup over the top of each donut. Serve immediately.

(10) Homemade Sugar Raised Donuts

This is a simple donut dish you can make whenever you are craving donuts, but don't want to make anything too complicated. It is so easy to make; these donuts can be made in just under 15 minutes.

Serving Sizes: 8 servings

Preparation Time: 15 minutes

Ingredients:

- ¼ cup of vegetable oil
- ½ cup of buttermilk
- 2 eggs, beaten
- ¾ cup of white sugar
- ½ teaspoon of salt
- 1 teaspoon of baking powder
- ½ teaspoon of pure vanilla
- 1 cup of all-purpose flour

Ingredients for the coating:

- ¼ cup of white sugar

||||||||||||||||||||||||||||||||||||||||||||||||||||||||||||||

Instructions:

1. Preheat the oven to 350 degrees. Grease a large donut pan with cooking spray.

2. In a large bowl, add in the vegetable oil, buttermilk, beaten eggs, white sugar, dash of salt, pure vanilla and baking powder. Add in the all-purpose flour, stir well until smooth in consistency.

3. Pour the batter into the prepared donut pan. Place into the oven to bake for 15 minutes. Remove and set the donuts onto a wire rack to cool completely.

4. Pour the ¼ cup of white sugar into a large Ziploc bag. Add in the donuts and shake until coated on all sides.

5. Place onto a serving platter and serve.

(11) Old Fashioned Cake Donuts

These delicious sour cream cake donuts are absolutely to die for. Soft on the inside and crispy on the outside, I know you will want to make these donuts as often as possible.

Serving Sizes: 12 servings

Preparation Time: 2 hours

Ingredients for the donuts:

- 1 ¼ cups of white sugar
- 2 ½ Tablespoon of butter, soft
- 5 egg yolks
- 1 ½ cups of sour cream
- 4 ¾ cup of all-purpose flour
- 1 Tablespoon + ¾ teaspoon of baking powder
- 1 Tablespoon of salt
- Canola oil, for frying

Ingredients for the glaze:

- ½ cup of whole milk
- 1 teaspoon of salt
- 3 ¼ cups of powdered sugar

||||||||||||||||||||||||||||||||||||||||||||||||||||||||||||||||

Instructions:

1. In a large bowl, add in the all-purpose flour and baking powder. Add in the salt and stir well until mixed. Set the mixture aside.

2. Line a large bowl with a sheet of plastic wrap and grease with cooking spray. Set the bowl aside.

3. In a large bowl of a stand mixer, add in the white sugar, soft butter and large egg yolks. Beat on the highest setting until creamy in consistency. Add in the sour cream and beat again until evenly mixed.

4. Add in the flour mixture and continue to beat until evenly incorporated.

5. Transfer the dough into the plastic lined bowl. Spray the dough with cooking spray and set into the fridge to chill for 1 hour.

6. Line a large baking sheet with a sheet of parchment paper. Grease with cooking spray. Dust a flat surface with some flour.

7. Place the dough onto the floured surface and dust the top of the dough with flour. Roll out the dough until ½ inch in thickness. Cut out each donut using a donut cutter and place onto the baking sheet. Cover and set into the fridge to chill for 30 minutes.

8. In a medium bowl, add in the whole milk, dash and powdered sugar. Whisk until smooth in consistency.

9. Pour 3 to 4 inches of canola oil into a large pot set over medium heat. Once the oil is shimmering, add in the donuts. Fry for 5 minutes or until golden brown. Remove and place onto a large plate lined with paper towels.

10. Once cooled, dunk the donuts in the glaze completely. Set onto a wire rack to set for 5 minutes before serving.

(12) Strawberry Donuts

If you love the fresh taste of strawberries, then this is one donut recipe I know you won't be able to get enough of. Packed full of a strawberry taste and smothered in a strawberry cream cheese frosting, this is a donut recipe the entire family will fall in love with.

Serving Sizes: 8 servings

Preparation Time: 20 minutes

Ingredients for the donuts:

- 1 cup of all-purpose flour
- 1/3 cup of sugar
- 1 teaspoon of baking powder
- ½ teaspoon of salt
- 1/3 cup of whole milk
- 1 egg, beaten
- 1 Tablespoon of butter, melted
- 1/3 cup of strawberries, chopped

Ingredients for the frosting:

- 2 ounces of cream cheese, soft
- 1 teaspoon of butter, melted
- 4 strawberries, pureed
- Dash of salt
- 1 ½ cups of powdered sugar

||||||||||||||||||||||||||||||||||||||||||||||||||||||||||||

Instructions:

1. In a large bowl, add in the all-purpose flour, dash of salt and baking powder. Stir well to mix.

2. In a separate small bowl, add in the whole milk, beaten egg, melted butter and chopped strawberries. Stir well to mix. Add this mixture to the flour mixture and stir well until just mixed.

3. Pour the batter into a large greased donut pan. Place into the oven to bake for 8 to 10 minutes at 425 degrees or until golden brown.

4. Remove and transfer the donuts onto a wire rack to cool completely.

5. In a small bowl, add in the cream cheese, melted butter, pureed strawberries, dash of salt and powdered sugar. Whisk until smooth in consistency.

6. Dip the tops of the donuts into the glaze. Serve.

(13) Baked Cinnamon Donuts

There is no other donut recipe that is quite as delicious as this one. These baked cinnamon donuts are topped off with a vanilla glaze, they are hard to resist.

Serving Sizes: 12 servings

Preparation Time: 25 minutes

Ingredients for the donuts:

- 1 cup of all-purpose flour
- ½ cup of white sugar
- 1 ½ teaspoon of baking powder
- ¼ teaspoon of salt
- ¼ teaspoon of ground cinnamon
- ½ cup of whole milk
- ½ teaspoon of white vinegar
- ½ teaspoon of pure vanilla
- 1 egg, beaten
- 4 tablespoons of butter, soft

Ingredients for the glaze:

- 2 tablespoons of whole milk
- ½ teaspoon of pure vanilla
- 1 cup of powdered sugar

IIIIIIIIIIIIIIIIIIIIIIIIIIIIIIIIIIIIIIIIIIIIIIIIIIIIIIIIIIIIIIIIIII

Instructions:

1. Preheat the oven to 350 degrees.

2. In a large bowl, add in the all-purpose flour, white sugar, dash of salt, ground cinnamon and baking powder. Stir well to mix.

3. In a small saucepan set over medium heat, add in the whole milk, vinegar, pure vanilla, beaten egg and soft butter. Stir well to mix. Add this mixture into the flour mixture. Stir well until just mixed.

4. Pour the batter into the donut pan. Place into the oven to bake for 12 to 15 minutes. Remove and place the donuts onto a wire rack to cool completely.

5. In a small saucepan set over medium heat, add in all of the ingredients for the glaze. Whisk until smooth in consistency. Remove from heat.

6. Dip the tops of the donuts in the glaze. Set back on the wire rack to set for 5 minutes before serving.

(14) Brownie and Cookie Donuts

These donuts are the perfect combination of both brownies and cookies. Packed full of a chocolatey taste, I know you will want to enjoy these donuts whenever you have the need to be spoiled.

Serving Sizes: 6 servings

Preparation Time: 30 minutes

Ingredients:

- 1, 18 box of brownie mix, including ingredients on the back
- 1, 8 ounce tub of cookie dough, crumbled
- 1, 6 ounce bar of chocolate, chopped
- 5 chocolate chip cookies, crumbled into crumbs

||||||||||||||||||||||||||||||||||||||||||||||||||||||||||||||||||

Instructions:

1. Preheat the oven to 350 degrees. Grease a large donut pan with cooking spray.

2. Prepare the brownie mix according to the directions on the package.

3. Pour the prepared brownie mixture into the greased donut pan.

4. Crumble the cookie dough over the batter.

5. Place into the oven to bake for 15 to 20 minutes or until baked through. Remove and set aside on a wire rack to cool completely.

6. In a small bowl, add the chopped chocolate. Cook in the microwave for 30 seconds or until melted. Drizzle the chocolate over the donuts.

7. Top off with the chocolate chip cookie crumbs and serve immediately.

(15) Baked Cinnamon and Sugar Donuts

This is the perfect donut dish to make to celebrate National Donut Day. In fact, these donuts are so taste, you will want to make them any day of the week.

Serving Sizes: 6 servings

Preparation Time: 25 minutes

Ingredients for the donuts:

- ¾ cup of all-purpose flour
- 2 tablespoons of cornstarch
- 1/3 cup of white sugar
- 1 teaspoon of baker's style baking powder
- ½ teaspoon of salt
- ½ teaspoon of ground cinnamon
- ¼ teaspoon of ground nutmeg
- 1/3 cup of buttermilk
- 1 egg, large
- 1 Tablespoon of butter, melted
- 1 teaspoon of pure vanilla

Ingredients for the topping:

- 3 tablespoons of butter, melted
- ½ cup of sugar + 1 teaspoon of ground cinnamon, mixed together

IIIIIIIIIIIIIIIIIIIIIIIIIIIIIIIIIIIIIIIIIIIIIIIIIIIIIIIIIIIIIIIIII

Instructions:

1. In a large bowl, add in the all-purpose flour, cornstarch, white sugar, ground nutmeg, ground cinnamon, dash of salt and baking powder. Stir well to mix.

2. In a small bowl, add in the buttermilk, large egg, butter and pure vanilla. Stir well to mix and pour into the flour mixture. Stir until just mixed.

3. Pour the batter into a large greased donut pan.

4. Place into the oven to bake for 12 to 15 minutes at 375 degrees or until baked through.

5. Remove and set onto a wire rack to cool completely.

6. Once cooled, brush the donuts with the three tablespoons of melted butter. Then transfer into a bowl with the sugar and cinnamon mixture. Toss to coat and serve immediately.

(16) S'mores Donuts

With the use of these delicious donuts, you won't have to go camping in order to enjoy authentic s'mores.

Serving Sizes: 6 servings

Preparation Time: 30 minutes

Ingredients for the donuts:

- 1 1/3 cup of yellow cake mix
- 1/3 cup of whole milk
- 1 Tablespoon of canola oil
- 1 egg, beaten

Ingredients for the frosting:

- 1 cup of powdered sugar
- ½ teaspoon of pure vanilla
- 1 Tablespoon of butter, soft
- 1/8 cup of water
- 1 cup of miniature marshmallows

Ingredients for the topping:

- ½ cup of semi-sweet chocolate chips
- 1 teaspoon of canola oil
- ½ cup of graham crackers, crushed

|||||||||||||||||||||||||||||||||||||||||||||||||||||||||||||||

Instructions:

1. Preheat the oven to 350 degrees. Grease a large donut pan with cooking spray.

2. In a large bowl, add in the yellow cake mix, whole milk, canola oil and beaten egg. Stir well until just mixed.

3. Pour the batter into the greased donut pan. Place into the oven to bake for 10 minutes. Remove and place the donuts onto a wire rack to cool completely.

4. In a small saucepan set over low to medium heat, add in the butter and water. Once the butter is melted, add in the miniature marshmallows and stir well until melted. Add in the pure vanilla and powdered sugar. Whisk until smooth in consistency.

5. Dip the tops of the donuts into the frosting and place back onto a wire rack to set.

6. In a small bowl, add in the chocolate chips. Melt the chocolate chips in the microwave. Add in the canola oil and stir well until smooth in consistency. Drizzle the chocolate over the top of the donuts.

7. Sprinkle the crushed graham crackers over the top of the donuts.

8. Server immediately.

(17) Funfetti Donuts

Make these special for those especially picky eaters in your home. Delicious glazed donuts topped off with rainbow sprinkles, these donuts are sure to brighten up anybody's day.

Serving Sizes: 8 servings

Preparation Time: 40 minutes

Ingredients for the donuts:

- 1 cup of all-purpose flour
- 1 teaspoon of baking powder
- ¼ teaspoon of baking soda
- ¼ teaspoon of ground nutmeg
- 1/3 cup of white sugar
- ¼ cup of whole milk
- ¼ cup of Greek yogurt
- 1 egg, beaten
- 2 tablespoons of unsalted butter, melted
- 1 ½ teaspoon of pure vanilla
- ½ cup of rainbow sprinkles

Ingredients for the glaze:

- ¼ cup of whole milk
- 2 cups of confectioner's sugar
- 1 teaspoon of pure vanilla
- Extra sprinkles, for topping and optional

||||||||||||||||||||||||||||||||||||||||||||||||||||||||||||||||

Instructions:

1. Preheat the oven to 350 degrees. Grease a large donut pan with cooking spray.

2. In a large bowl, add in the all-purpose flour, ground nutmeg, white sugar, baking powder and soda. Stir well until evenly mixed.

3. In a separate medium bowl, add in the whole milk, yogurt and beaten egg. Whisk until smooth in consistency. Add in the melted butter and pure vanilla. Whisk again until mixed. Add this mixture into the flour mixture and stir until just mixed.

4. Pour the batter into the greased donut pan. Place into the oven to bake for 8 to 10 minutes or until golden brown. Remove and place the donuts onto a wire rack to cool completely.

5. In a medium saucepan set over low heat, add in all of the ingredients for the glaze. Whisk until smooth in consistency. Remove immediately from heat.

6. Dip the tops of the donuts into the glaze and set back onto the wire rack to set.

7. Sprinkle the rainbow sprinkles over the top and serve.

(18) Chai Spiced Donuts

If you love the taste of classic Chai Tea, then this is the perfect donut recipe for you to prepare. It is perfect to make for those who need to follow strict diets.

Serving Sizes: 10 servings

Preparation Time: 25 minutes

Ingredients for the donuts:

- 6 eggs, beaten
- ½ cup of coconut flour
- ½ cup of sweetener
- ¼ cup of avocado oil
- 1 teaspoon of lemon juice
- ½ teaspoon of baking soda
- Dash of sea salt
- 2 teaspoons of pure vanilla
- 2 teaspoons of ground cinnamon
- 1 teaspoon of ginger
- 1 teaspoon of cardamom
- ½ teaspoon of ground cloves
- ¼ teaspoon of grated nutmeg
- Dash of black pepper

Ingredients for the icing:

- 1/3 cup of coconut oil
- 3 tablespoons of maple sugar
- ½ teaspoon of pure vanilla
- ¼ to ½ teaspoon of grated nutmeg

|||||||||||||||||||||||||||||||||||||||||||||||||||||||||

Instructions:

1. Preheat the oven to 350 degrees. Grease a large donut pan with cooking spray.

2. In a large bowl, add in all of the ingredients for the donuts. Stir well until just mixed.

3. Pour the batter into the greased donut pan. Place into the oven to bake for 15 to 20 minutes or until baked through. Remove and transfer the donuts onto a wire rack to cool completely.

4. In a double boiler set over medium heat, add in the coconut oil. Once melted, add in the maple sugar. Whisk until smooth in consistency.

5. Drizzle the glaze over the donuts. Set aside for 5 minutes to set before serving.

(19) Coffee Cake Donuts

This is a delicious donut recipe you can prepare whenever you want to impress your friends and family with your baking skills.

Serving Sizes: 6 servings

Preparation Time: 30 minutes

Ingredients for the topping:

- ¼ cup of unsalted butter, melted
- ¼ cup of light brown sugar
- 1 cup of all-purpose flour
- ½ teaspoon of ground cinnamon

Ingredients for the donuts:

- 1 cup of all-purpose flour
- 1 teaspoon of baking powder
- ½ teaspoon of salt
- ¼ cup of white sugar
- 1 egg, large
- 1 Tablespoon of unsalted butter
- ½ cup of whole milk
- 1 teaspoon of pure vanilla

Ingredients for the glaze:

- ½ cup of confectioner's sugar
- ½ Tablespoon of whole milk

llllllllllllllllllllllllllllllllllllllllllllllllllllllllll

Instructions:

1. Preheat the oven to 325 degrees. Grease a large donut pan with cooking spray and set aside.

2. In a large bowl, add in the melted butter. Add in the brown sugar, 1 cup of all-purpose flour and ground cinnamon. Stir well until crumbly. Set the mixture aside.

3. In a separate medium bowl, add in the all-purpose flour, baking powder and dash of salt. Stir well to mix and set the mixture aside.

4. In a large bowl of a stand mixer, Add in the white sugar, large egg and melted butter. Add in the whole milk and pure vanilla. Beat on the medium setting until evenly mixed. Add in the flour mixture and continue to beat until evenly incorporated.

5. Pour the batter into the greased donut pan.

6. Place into the oven to bake for 15 to 17 minutes or until the donuts are golden brown. Remove and transfer the donuts onto a large wire rack to cool completely.

7. In a medium bowl, add in the whole milk and powdered sugar. Whisk until smooth in consistency.

8. Drizzle the glaze over the donuts and top off with the crumb topping. Serve.

(20) Glazed Maple Donuts

These are simple donuts that are the perfect treat to serve for breakfast. Made with a thick and sweet maple glaze, I know you won't be able to get enough of these donuts.

Serving Sizes: 8 servings

Preparation Time: 45 minutes

Ingredients for the glaze:

- ¼ cup of butter, soft
- ½ cup of pure maple syrup
- 1 cup of confectioner's sugar
- ½ teaspoon of maple extract, optional

Ingredients for the donuts:

- 1 cup of all-purpose flour
- 1 teaspoon of baker's style baking powder
- ¼ teaspoon of baker's style baking soda
- 1 teaspoon of ground cinnamon
- ½ teaspoon of ground nutmeg
- ¼ teaspoon of ground cloves
- ¼ teaspoon of salt
- 1 egg, beaten
- 1/3 cup of light brown sugar
- ¼ cup of whole milk
- ¼ cup of plain yogurt
- 2 tablespoons of butter, melted
- 1 ½ teaspoon of pure vanilla

IIIIIIIIIIIIIIIIIIIIIIIIIIIIIIIIIIIIIIIIIIIIIIIIIIIIIIIIIIIIIIIIII

Instructions:

1. In a small saucepan set over low heat, add in the butter and maple syrup. Whisk to mix and once melted, remove from heat. Add in the confectioner's sugar and whisk until smooth in consistency. Set the glaze aside to thicken.

2. Preheat the oven to 350 degrees. Grease a large donut pan with cooking spray.

3. In a medium bowl, add in the all-purpose flour, ground cinnamon, ground nutmeg, cloves, dash of salt, baking powder and soda. Add in the beaten egg, light brown sugar, whole milk and plain yogurt. Stir again to mix.

4. Add in the melted butter and pure vanilla. Stir again until just mixed.

5. Pour the batter into the greased donut pan. Place into the oven to bake for 8 to 10 minutes or until golden. Remove and place the donuts onto a wire rack to cool completely.

6. Dip the tops of the donuts into the glaze. Place back onto the wire rack to set for 5 minutes before serving.

(21) Baked Oatmeal Donuts

These donuts are perfect to make for those who suffer from sensitive tummies. Made with a sweet maple glaze, these donuts are one you won't be able to get enough of.

Serving Sizes: 12 servings

Preparation Time: 20 minutes

Ingredients for the donuts:

- 1 ¼ cups of whole wheat flour
- ¾ cup of oat flour
- ¾ cup of light brown sugar
- 2 teaspoons of baking powder
- 1 teaspoon of salt
- ½ teaspoon of nutmeg, grated
- ¼ teaspoon of ground cinnamon
- ¾ cup of whole milk
- 2 eggs, beaten
- 1 teaspoon of pure vanilla

Ingredients for the glaze:

- 1 cup of powdered sugar
- 2 tablespoons of maple syrup
- 1 teaspoon of pure vanilla
- Dash of salt

|||||||||||||||||||||||||||||||||||||||||||||||||||||||||||||||

Instructions:

1. Preheat the oven to 325 degrees. Grease a large donut pan with cooking spray.

2. In a large bowl, add in the whole wheat flour, oat flour, grated nutmeg, ground cinnamon, teaspoon of salt, light brown sugar and baking powder. Stir well until evenly mixed.

3. In a separate medium bowl, add in the whole milk, beaten eggs and pure vanilla. Whisk until blended and pour into the flour mixture. Stir until just mixed.

4. Pour the donut batter into the greased donut pan. Place into the oven to bake for 8 to 10 minutes or until the donuts are golden. Remove and place the donuts onto a wire rack to cool completely.

5. In a medium bowl, add in all of the ingredients for the glaze. Whisk until smooth in consistency.

6. Dip the tops of the donuts in the glaze. Set back onto the wire rack to set for 10 minutes before serving.

(22) Banana Bread Donuts with a Caramel Glaze

If you love the taste of classic banana bread, then this is the perfect donut recipe for you to prepare. Smothered in a brown butter and caramel glaze, these donuts are perfect to serve during the holiday season.

Serving Sizes: 6 donuts

Preparation Time: 30 minutes

Ingredients for the donuts:

- 1 egg, beaten
- ½ cup of light brown sugar
- ¼ cup of white sugar
- ¼ cup of vegetable oil
- ¼ cup of sour cream
- 2 teaspoons of pure vanilla
- 1 cup of ripe bananas, mashed
- 1 ¼ cups of all-purpose flour
- ½ teaspoon of baking powder
- ½ teaspoon of baking soda
- ¼ teaspoon of salt

Ingredients for the glaze:

- ¼ cup of unsalted butter, browned
- 1/3 cup of light brown sugar
- 3 tablespoons of half and half
- 2 cups of confectioner's sugar
- ½ teaspoon of pure vanilla
- ¼ teaspoon of salt, optional

||||||||||||||||||||||||||||||||||||||||||||||||||||||||||||||||||

Instructions:

1. Preheat the oven to 350 degrees. Grease a large donut pan with cooking spray.

2. In a large bowl, add in the beaten egg, light brown sugar, white sugar, vegetable oil, sour cream and pure vanilla. Whisk until evenly mixed. Add in the mashed bananas and stir well to mix.

3. Add in the all-purpose flour, dash of salt, baking powder and soda. Stir until just mixed.

4. Pour the batter into the prepared donut pan. Place into the oven to bake for 12 to 15 minutes or until cooked through. Remove and place onto a wire rack to cool completely.

5. Place a medium saucepan over medium heat to high heat. Add in the butter and cook for 5 to 10 minutes or until the butter is brown. Add in the light brown sugar and whisk until smooth. Continue to cook for an additional minute. Remove from heat and set aside to cool for 1 minute.

6. Add in the half and half, pure vanilla and dash of salt. Add in the powdered sugar and whisk until smooth in consistency.

7. Dip the tops of the donuts into the glaze. Set back onto a wire rack to set for 5 minutes before serving.

(23) Pumpkin Spiced Donuts

This is the perfect donut recipe to make right in time for the fall season. Moist and bursting with a pumpkin flavor, these donuts are hard to resist.

Serving Sizes: 10 servings

Preparation Time: 25 minutes

Ingredients for the donuts:

- 1 cup of pumpkin, pureed
- 2 eggs, beaten lightly
- ¼ cup of pumpkin spice creamer
- ¼ cup of coconut oil
- 1 teaspoon of pure vanilla
- 2 cups of all-purpose flour
- ¼ cup of white sugar
- ½ cup of light brown sugar
- 2 teaspoons of baker's style baking powder
- ¼ teaspoon of baker's style baking soda
- 2 teaspoons of pumpkin pie spice
- ½ teaspoon of salt

Ingredients for the glaze:

- ¼ cup of butter, soft
- ¼ cup of maple syrup
- 2 tablespoons of pumpkin pie spice creamer
- 1 teaspoon of maple extract
- 1 1/3 cups of powdered sugar

||||||||||||||||||||||||||||||||||||||||||||||||||||||||||||

Instructions:

1. Preheat the oven to 325 degrees. Grease a large donut pan with cooking spray.

2. In a large bowl, add in the pureed pumpkin, beaten eggs, ¼ cup of pumpkin spice creamer, coconut oil and pure vanilla. Stir well to mix.

3. In a separate large bowl, add in the all-purpose flour, white sugar, light brown sugar, pumpkin pie spice, dash of salt, baking powder and soda.

4. Add the flour mixture into the pumpkin mixture. Stir well until just mixed.

5. Pour the batter into the prepared donut pan. Place into the oven to bake for 12 to 15 minutes or until golden brown. Remove and transfer the donuts onto a wire rack to cool completely.

6. In a small saucepan set over medium heat, add in the butter, maple syrup and two tablespoons of pumpkin pie spice creamer. Stir well until evenly mixed and cook until the butter is melted. Add in the maple extract and powdered sugar. Whisk until smooth in consistency. Remove from heat.

7. Dip the tops of the donuts into the glaze. Set back onto the wire rack to set for 5 minutes before serving.

(24) Oreo Donuts

If you love the taste of Oreos, then this is the perfect donut recipe for you to prepare. There are Oreos in the donut batter and in the topping, this is the perfect donut dish for the Oreo addict.

Serving Sizes: 6 servings

Preparation Time: 45 minutes

Ingredients:

- 1 cup of all-purpose flour
- 3 tablespoons of white sugar
- 1 teaspoon of baking powder
- ½ teaspoon of salt
- 6 tablespoons of whole milk
- 1 egg, beaten
- ½ teaspoon of pure vanilla
- 3 tablespoons of vegetable oil
- 9 Oreos, chopped
- 5 to 6 Oreos, crumbled and for topping
- 2 to 3 pieces of white chocolate, finely chopped

|||||||||||||||||||||||||||||||||||||||||||||||||||||||||||||||||||||||

Instructions:

1. Preheat the oven to 325 degrees. Grease a large donut pan with cooking spray.

2. In a large bowl, add in the all-purpose flour, white sugar, baking powder and dash of salt. Stir well to mix.

3. In a separate large bowl, add in the whole milk, beaten egg, pure vanilla and vegetable oil. Stir well to mix and pour into the flour mixture. Stir well until just mixed.

4. Add in the 9 chopped Oreos and fold gently to incorporate.

5. Pour the batter into the prepared donut pan. Place into the oven to bake for 10 minutes or until baked through. Remove and place the donuts onto a wire rack to cool completely.

6. Melt the white chocolate in a small bowl. Dip each of the donuts into the melted chocolate. Set aside to harden for 2 to 5 minutes.

7. Dip the donuts into the crumbled Oreos and serve.

(25) Sweet Honey Donuts

This is the perfect donut recipe to prepare if you have a strong sweet tooth that needs to be satisfied. Be sure to use the freshest honey for the tastiest results.

Serving Sizes: 10 to 12 servings

Preparation Time: 18 minutes

Ingredients for the donuts:

- 1 ¾ cup of all-purpose flour
- 1 ½ teaspoon of baking powder
- ½ teaspoon of baking soda
- Dash of salt
- ½ teaspoon of ground cinnamon
- ½ cup of white sugar
- 2 eggs, beaten
- ¾ cup of buttermilk
- 3 tablespoons of butter, melted
- ¼ cup of honey
- 1 teaspoon of pure vanilla
- 2 tablespoons of sour cream

Ingredients for the glaze:

- 1 cup of powdered sugar
- 2 tablespoons of heavy whipping cream
- 2 tablespoons of honey

IIIIIIIIIIIIIIIIIIIIIIIIIIIIIIIIIIIIIIIIIIIIIIIIIIIIIIIIIIIIIII

Instructions:

1. Preheat the oven to 350 degrees. Grease a large donut pan with cooking spray.

2. In a large bowl, add in the beaten eggs, white sugar, buttermilk, sour cream, butter, honey and pure vanilla. Whisk until smooth in consistency.

3. Add in the all-purpose flour, dash of salt, ground cinnamon, white sugar, baking powder and soda. Stir well until just mixed.

4. Pour the batter into the greased donut pan. Place into the oven to bake for 10 to 12 minutes or until light gold. Remove and place the donuts onto a wire rack to cool completely.

5. In a small bowl, add in the powdered sugar, heavy cream and honey. Whisk until smooth in consistency.

6. Drizzle the glaze over the tops of the donuts. Set aside to set for 5 minutes before serving.

About the Author

Nancy Silverman is an accomplished chef from Essex, Vermont. Armed with her degree in Nutrition and Food Sciences from the University of Vermont, Nancy has excelled at creating e-books that contain healthy and delicious meals that anyone can make and everyone can enjoy. She improved her cooking skills at the New England Culinary Institute in Montpelier Vermont and she has been working at perfecting her culinary style since graduation. She claims that her life's work is always a work in progress and she only hopes to be an inspiration to aspiring chefs everywhere.

Her greatest joy is cooking in her modern kitchen with her family and creating inspiring and delicious meals. She often says that she has perfected her signature dishes based on her family's critique of each and every one.

Nancy has her own catering company and has also been fortunate enough to be head chef at some of Vermont's most exclusive restaurants. When a friend suggested she share some of her outstanding signature dishes, she decided to add cookbook author to her repertoire of personal achievements. Being a technological savvy woman, she felt the e-book realm would be a better fit and soon she had her first cookbook available online. As of today, Nancy has sold over 1,000 e-books and has shared her culinary experiences and brilliant recipes with people from all over the world! She plans on expanding into self-help books and dietary cookbooks, so stayed tuned!

Author's Afterthoughts

Thank you for making the decision to invest in one of my cookbooks! I cherish all my readers and hope you find joy in preparing these meals as I have.

There are so many books available and I am truly grateful that you decided to buy this one and follow it from beginning to end.

I love hearing from my readers on what they thought of this book and any value they received from reading it. As a personal favor, I would appreciate any feedback you can give in the form of a review on Amazon and please be honest! This kind of support will help others make an informed choice on and will help me tremendously in producing the best quality books possible.

My most heartfelt thanks,

Nancy Silverman

If you're interested in more of my books, be sure to follow my author page on Amazon (can be found on the link Bellow) or scan the QR-Code.

https://www.amazon.com/author/nancy-silverman

Printed by Amazon Italia Logistica S.r.l.
Torrazza Piemonte (TO), Italy